Learn to Find Your
Creative Self...Quickly

Janet Scarpone

Balboa Press books may be ordered through booksellers or by contacting:

Balboa Press
A Division of Hay House
1663 Liberty Drive
Bloomington, IN 47403
www.balboapress.com
1 (877) 407-4847

ISBN: 978-1-5043-8138-3 (sc)
ISBN: 978-1-5043-8139-0 (e)

Print information available on the last page.

Balboa Press rev. date: 04/13/2018

I would like to dedicate ***Learn to Find Your Creative Self... Quickly*** *to all of my students, past and present. I would like to thank all of my associates for their constant support. May everyone who goes on this adventure learn quickly!*

Janet Scarpone

Contents

An Introduction

Are you ready for some self-exploration? As a communication professor, getting to know my subject, myself, and my students (not necessarily in that order) has been the centerpiece of my life. I have read so many books on communication outside of academia that have been wonderful journeys for me. I wanted to engage others to learn about themselves and to make life changes while encouraging and building their self-esteem in an entire class centered on **intrapersonal communication** or communication with self. It began with an independent study hybrid class which worked quite well. Then I put it all online and it worked even better! My students were meeting and enjoying their creative selves and, consequently, changing their own lives. Now it is also in a workbook format along with a video called *Dreams Can Come True* and it was made just for you.

This twelve-week adventure is designed to build more positive feelings towards ourselves. No matter how high a person's self-esteem is, isn't it fun to know it can always go higher? As each person learns more about his or her wonderful creative self, self-esteem grows. Then, as each person becomes more positive and self-accepting, so does his or her life. What we think about, we generate more of. What are you thinking about regularly? What are you dreaming about? Are you retelling the tales of your old negative life events over and over again or are you talking about your new positive life dreams? It makes a difference, you know. That self-fulfilling prophecy comes into play. If you are worrying about something, haven't you noticed that it often comes to pass? And conversely, the more expectant you are of good things, the more those come to pass.

Learning to find your creative self is an adventure made just for you. Does the adventure ever stop? No, it continues each and every day of our lives. Abraham Lincoln once said, "Most folks are as happy as they make up their minds to be." How happy do you want to be? Are you ready to reach your own personal "happiness best"? Why not try? Intrapersonal communication continues every day as long as we are alive and kicking. The more positive we feel about ourselves, the more successful the day becomes. The more positive we feel about life and living, the smoother our communication becomes and the happier our lives become.

I have lived a long time and I have read many, many books and experienced many varied life adventures. I have studied under many fine teachers. However, there is a master teacher—a master creator, if you will—inside us all who has something to say. If you don't let that creative self have its voice, there will probably be some angst in your life. I'm letting my creative self speak in this book—in the life lessons, in the choice of questions, and in this introduction for you.

This is very easy to follow. Each week you read a life lesson, answer the questions, take a fun play date by yourself, find fifteen minutes a day to relax, and write three pages on three different days in your journal. The more you concentrate on building positive times in your week, the better you will feel and the more those positive feelings will multiply and seep into other areas.

We all have such busy lives and schedules. I have endeavored to make this light and tight. Beginning to make changes to attitudes and beliefs takes time and energy. Space is needed to create. By reading a book like this, we are creating a new chapter in our lives.

We don't need bitterness and misery to create. We don't need to be verbally abused or beaten to perform better. We don't need to be alcohol drenched or to ingest massive amounts of drugs to create whatever masterpieces we want to give to the world. Creativity flourishes in an atmosphere of love and respect and encouragement. Forget the negative past. Focus on building a positive present and future. To find one's creative self does not have to be a difficult and unpleasant task. It can be joyous and fun. Oh my, having fun while learning—my favorite! That's why I became a teacher. I love communication experiences that bring joy to our hearts, don't you? This one has the added benefit of building self-love at the same time. How could it get any better than that?

Here is the list of the life lessons:

1. Journaling, Play Dates, and More
2. Intrapersonal Communication Basics: The Self
3. More Self-Exploration
4. Vitality
5. Acceptance and Success
6. Imagination, Enthusiasm, Hope

7. Self-Trust and Future Goals
8. Dreaming
9. Abundance
10. Appreciation
11. More Self-Awareness
12. Final Overview and Ending Thoughts

Remember that this book encourages positive communication with yourself. Below is my list of the basic competencies; however, often participants report learning even more.

1. Journal often to discover inner desires and goals.
2. Research creative options in life.
3. Improve inner relationship with self.
4. Explore self-concept and self-esteem issues while improving self-perception and attitude.
5. Explore creative options to blocked areas.
6. Clear out barriers to goals through appreciation.
7. Acquire a more positive attitude towards self-exploration.
8. Demonstrate the ability to find, enjoy, and utilize creative outlets.
9. Communicate clearly and logically when answering lesson questions.
10. Critically think about and evaluate life choices.
11. Read, analyze, and apply these lessons to new situations.
12. Identify goals that lead to hope, trust, vitality, and success.

Enjoy every minute of your adventure.

All my best,

Janet Scarpone

Life Lesson 1

Life Lesson 1

Journaling, Play Dates, and More

Is creativity natural? You bet it is. Life is basically full of wonderful creative energy. Refusing or denying creativity just goes against the grain. Telling yourself that dreams don't matter and that you shouldn't imagine what you want in life effectively turns the inner you off. And it doesn't matter what others might think of your creative plans or ideas. After all, creativity is not an extra-curricular activity in life. It shouldn't be thought of as something extra you get to experience occasionally. Creativity is what feeds your spirit.

A good way to find out who you are as a creative person is to keep a journal. In this book I am asking you to write three pages, in long-hand, in a journal on three days a week preferably as soon as you wake up. Please use a stream-of-consciousness format, a most effective tool to help you get in touch with your own creative self. These pages are not supposed to be polished. **Do not** check for spelling or grammar mistakes, or whether you "sound smart." Just go with the flow. Perhaps you will write about what a great day you have ahead of you. Perhaps you will write the answers to the "Questions to Ponder" in each lesson. Perhaps you will write about the date you had the night before or something fun you did or are going to do. Perhaps you just want to gripe about something. Go for it! Whatever comes to you—just write it down. Even if nothing particular comes to you, write about that. Eventually, as you let your creative self emerge, more and more will come to the surface. You will get the hang of it all once you start doing it.

No-one is allowed to read these pages. Even you should not reread them—yet! I will, however, occasionally ask you to mark off a paragraph to share as part of a life lesson. Later on, down the line, there will be a very important exercise where you will utilize these pages. You are on your honor to do this. Plus you don't want to miss out on the benefits of that future, important exercise. It will be your final overview. Resist rereading; just make a commitment with yourself to write three pages, preferably as soon as you wake up, three times a week. The more you write, the more the stuff that stands in the way of your creativity is erased. Commit yourself to these rules: No criticizing! No judging! Just write whatever crosses your mind. Writing is a way to accept where we are in our lives, a way to encourage inner creativity to appear. Actually, the more you write, the more you can find yourself beginning to focus on non-stressful activities; hence, the less stressed you will be.

In order to allow the new into your life, it helps to clear away the old. Here are some fun ideas/alternatives that can help with this section. Occasionally, you could try different approaches to these pages:

a. Write in very large letters.
b. Scribble.
c. Doodle.
d. Paint.
e. Draw pictures instead.
f. Type them on your computer. (Just keep in mind that long-hand writing can be a better connection with the inner you.)
g. Put on a timer for ten minutes and write very, very quickly so that you are finished before the timer rings. Make sure you focus.
h. Speak into a recorder when you need a change from writing.
i. Better yet—sing or rap or rhyme or chant your thoughts.
j. Write later on in the day if you didn't get a chance in the morning.
k. Write with different colored crayons or markers.
l. Write in letter format. Pick someone wonderful to write to in your imagination.
m. Write in bullet format.

Above all, begin to look forward to writing and try to make it fun!

Also, every week, find a block of time—preferably a few hours—especially for you. It's a play date that you make with yourself. ***Alone.*** As you spend quality time with your inner self, you will get to know yourself better. It's an exercise in intrapersonal communication—communication with the self. It helps you to become more intimate with you. You don't want to miss out on this!

In addition to writing three pages three days a week and making a weekly date with yourself for twelve weeks, you can also write once a week the answers to the questions at the end of the life lessons. This is not something that you can leave until the end and cram to finish. It is best to do this step-by-step for twelve weeks giving yourself one week to complete each lesson.

These life lessons, including your personal writings and comments, are "classified" and confidential. Do not send them to anyone else. The materials are just for you and the lessons need to be done in a special sequence which depends on you and your goals and abilities. Each person is unique and has a unique path.

If you are using this program in an academic situation that calls for a supplementary book, may I suggest *Orbiting the Giant Hairball: A Corporate Fool's Guide to Surviving with Grace* by Gordon MacKenzie. There are twenty-four chapters. I would suggest reading two or three chapters each week with your concentration on what are you relating to the most in each chapter. Then, look to complete the Book Reflections included in Life Lesson 10.

There's one more item to incorporate into your creativity renewal list. Please find about fifteen minutes each day for some quiet time just for you. Make this a time for you to relax and clear the slate for fifteen minutes. Even if you are exceptionally busy, you could look for five minute intervals throughout the day. This is your downtime, just for you. Shut the door. Relax. Rejuvenate. Renew. If it's possible, lie down and dream of lovely adventures. If you like to meditate, this would be a good time to do that. Find a way to clear your mind so that you can refresh yourself. Fifteen minutes a day of downtime just for you.

Remember, start writing three pages on three separate days, make a play date with yourself this week, and give yourself a break every day. Also remember to use your imagination! This adventure does need your truthfulness. As you write from the heart, do remember to be thorough with your lesson answers. Don't leave anything out! There are no right or wrong answers.

There are also some group discussion questions at the end of each life lesson that you can answer each week. Remember, when we really start getting in touch with our creative selves, we begin to see others who are doing similar things. It's fun to also be able to connect in a group situation, if possible.

The *Dreams Can Come True* video was made especially for you. The best time to begin watching it is after reading the video introduction in Life Lesson 8. However, feel free to watch and enjoy it at any time. Please do visit www.learnquickly.com/creativeself.htm for even more information.

These life lessons evolved from my own creative adventures and from reading a variety of materials from many different authors over the years. Some of these specialists include: Ron Adler, James Allen, Julie Cameron, Joseph Campbell, Jack Canfield, Dr. Wayne Dyer, Emmett Fox, Shakti Gawain, Louise Hay, Jerry and Esther Hicks, Napoleon Hill, Ernest Holmes, Mark Knapp, Alan Lakein, Gordon MacKenzie, Stefan Murnaw, Wendy Oldfield, Catherine Ponder, and Neil Towne among others. My own education, life experiences, and the experiences of others have helped me to create this book. I hope you enjoy it!

Every week I will ask you to write your answers to specific questions. Below is the first set of **Questions to Answer**:

1. How many days this week did you write three pages in your journal? I'm hoping that three is your answer. Briefly describe your topics. Did you enjoy writing in your journal? Is there anything you were surprised that you were writing about? Don't worry if what you are writing about seems odd or strange or trivial. Let your creative self begin to emerge and let the writing flow. Journaling helps you to take your own emotional temperature rather than measuring your progress.

2. What did you do on your play date by yourself this week? Did you have fun? I certainly hope so. Play time is an important and necessary part of our lives. We often don't make enough time for ourselves. People from other countries often criticize us Americans for not taking enough time out for ourselves—for not taking time to smell the roses. Don't let your life slip by without enjoying it. Don't forget your weekly play date. Start looking forward to each one. What will you do next week?

3. Were you able to take fifteen minutes of complete and total relaxation just for you each day? How many days this week did you do that?

4. I would like you to draw a self-portrait now. If you are like me, you will be drawing a stick figure. This does not have to take a lot of time and it does not have to be a major work of art. Just draw a picture of yourself here. We will come back to this drawing at the end of the book. Did you draw it?

Please choose 8 out of the next 10 to answer:

5. Did anything happen this week that surprised or inspired you in a special way?

6. Are you aware of old feelings, ideas, or beliefs that stand in the way of you reaching your personal best? Please list ten of them and decide if you are willing to keep the focus off of them for the next several weeks.

7. What positive feelings, ideas, or beliefs could you substitute for your list from question 6? Make sure these are possible substitutions. If you want to substitute excitement for fear but you know that's a long shot, aim for a feeling like hope instead. Please make a new list as you cross off the old list.

8. Who are three or four people who believe in you and your ability to create? Please list them. What kinds of things have they done or said to you that made you feel that way? You may want to write out some of those kind words and read them each day. My best friend is on my list. She always tells me something nice about me. Who is on your list?

9. Write a list of ten items that you appreciate about you. Before you go to sleep at night, think of things that happened during the day that you loved. When you wake up in the morning, think about them again. Appreciate yourself. This week remember to read each day that list of ten items that you like about yourself.

10. If you could have five other jobs, what would they be and why? Are there any aspects of these jobs that you could incorporate into your life right now? For instance, I would have loved to have been an athlete so I exercise every day. If you would have liked to have been a doctor, perhaps you enjoy reading medical journals.

11. Name five things that you love about your life or about life in general.

12. Write another list of what is wonderful about you. How many more items can you list? Can you make it at least ten more? Put that list somewhere you will see it every day.

13. You have been given three wishes just for you and no-one else. What do you wish for yourself and why?

14. When do you allow the creative part of you to come out and play? What kinds of things keep that from happening in your life?

At the end of each lesson I have included questions for either group discussion or for individual use and some questions for you to ponder.

Questions for Discussion:

A. Introduce yourself. Who are you? Include the URL to your favorite video and describe why that video represents some part of you and/or why you like it.

B. If you could have a date with anyone—ANYONE (dead or alive)—who would it be and why? Where would you go? What would you do?

C. What was your favorite childhood game? What was so great about it? Would you still play it now? What feelings does it bring up for you?

D. If you could go anywhere in the world, where would you go and why?

Here are some more questions for you to think about or perhaps you would like to answer them in your journal.

Questions to Ponder:

What's so fun about being creative?

What would you do over again in your life if you could?

What would you do differently?

What do you appreciate about your own brand of creativity?

Who else appreciates that part of you?

When do you have the most fun?

What do you especially appreciate about yourself?

What other play date ideas do you have in mind?

Do you have a special place to put your journal?

What do you love about having time just for yourself?

Have you searched for any video clips or movies to watch on creativity?

Life Lesson 2

Life Lesson 2

The Self

How aware of you are you? As we watch ourselves interacting with others, we often compare ourselves to them. If the comparison is with someone we respect and is positive, we pat ourselves on the backs. If we compare ourselves negatively, it doesn't feel so good. In this life lesson, I'm going to propose some "food for thought" questions regarding your concept of your **Self**. After you read the lesson, allow your thoughts to just "drift" awhile before you try to come up with your answers.

In general, what is your perception of yourself? What kind of a person do you see yourself as being? How do you feel about you? What do you think about yourself? Your attitudes, your values, and your beliefs are what form this concept of self. These attitudes, values, and beliefs are deeply rooted and are often slow to change. But we don't have to do it slowly. Keep in mind that beliefs are formed by the habitual thinking of the same thought or thoughts about a topic. In other words—a practiced thought. You can always decide to change the thought and that will change the belief. Whenever you can replace negative habitual thoughts with positive habitual thoughts, your self-concept (your perception of yourself) gets a boost.

Others influence how we perceive ourselves. When we think that loved and respected family and friends love and respect us in return, it makes us feel good. However, if family and friends think negatively about us and we care about their opinions, it doesn't make us feel so good. When we feel bad about ourselves and have a poor self-concept, those negative "vibes" definitely impact how we interact with others.

If you are not who you want to be, can you get closer and closer to becoming your ideal? Of course you can. Old habitual habits of thought can be turned around. You are in the process of doing that right now by raising your own self-esteem or how you value yourself.

Self-love is the answer. Can you lovingly accept where you are at right now as you begin to self-soothe and nurture yourself? Doing this will help you to reach your own personal best. Can you see a glass half-full rather than half-empty? It just takes some persistent but kind and loving practice.

How does your best friend treat you? How do you like to be treated? It's time to treat yourself like you are your own best friend. Truly, how kind are you to yourself? What kind thoughts have you been thinking lately? How nice are you to others? How nice are you to you?

Telling our personal information to others is called self-disclosure. How much do you reveal to others? When? Why? How often? To whom? Has self-disclosure brought you closer to others or farther away?

Remember that the self-concept is your own perception of yourself. This begins to develop when you, as a child, start to become aware of yourself. Can you change your self-concept? Yes. How would you do that, if you wanted to? Self-esteem is the value you give to yourself. How are you feeling about yourself right now?

Have you heard the term self-fulfilling prophecy? A self-fulfilling prophecy happens when you expect something to happen and it does. Some believe you get more of what you give your attention to. So, if you give your attention to stress and problems, you get more of them. On the other hand, if you give your attention to appreciation and kindness, you get more of that. What are you choosing to notice?

I believe in this idea of imagining what you want to happen before it happens. It's the opposite of worrying. With worry we are planning for the negative. With imagining what we want to happen, we are planning for the positive. When you believe something can happen, the chances of it actually happening increase. It's that idea of the self-fulfilling prophecy. If you think you can pass the test and you study hard, you probably will. The opposite is true, also. If you don't think you can pass the test, even if you study hard, you just might not. Your belief system might not let you. So why not imagine what you want happening?

One of my students during my second year of teaching communication put it very succinctly. He said, "It's like what the football coach always tells us, 'If you believe you can do it, you can do it. If you don't believe you can do it, you'll probably never do it.'" He believed what his coach had to say. What are your beliefs these days? They are especially important in an adventure like this.

I've posed many questions in this life lesson. Again, let them "settle in" a bit before you dive into the lesson questions.

Questions to Answer:

1. Did you write in your journal three times this week? How many pages did you write each time? Were there any big revelations?

2. Did you take a play date? What did you do? On a scale of 1-10 with 10 being the most fun, how much fun was it?

3. Were you able to take fifteen minutes of complete and total relaxation just for you each day? How many days this week did you do that?

4. Did you make a self-portrait last week? This can be a stick figure. I will be asking you to do something with this at the end of the book.

Please choose 8 out of the next 10 to answer:

5. Did anything happen this week that surprised or inspired you in a special way?

6. Who is one person to whom you compare yourself favorably? How are you similar?

7. What kind of a person are you? In what areas do you want to grow and expand?

8. Are you your own best friend? Write a few examples describing how you treat yourself on a daily basis. How can you become closer and nicer to you?

9. To whom do you tell your secrets? Describe a situation where that worked out well for you. How do you decide to whom you will tell your secrets? How do you decide how much and what to reveal?

10. What areas of your self-concept would you like to change? What negative beliefs could you change into positive beliefs? How would you do that?

11. How are you feeling about yourself right now? On a scale of 1-10 with 10 being the best, rate how you felt yesterday morning, afternoon, late afternoon, and evening. Did you hold steady at one number or was it up and down? Why?

12. What is one thing you could do right now that would help you to reach a higher "feel good" number?

13. What is the nicest thing that anyone has ever said to you? How often do you say that to yourself?

14. If they made a movie of your life, who would you like to see play you in the movie? Why?

Questions for Discussion:

A. Describe your best friend. What is he or she like?

B. What is your favorite book and/or movie? Why?

C. What is your favorite dinner? Describe it in detail from soup to nuts! Where would you most want to eat it and with whom?

D. What is a belief you have that serves you well?

Questions to Ponder:

Who are you?

What do you think is your purpose in life?

How much do you like yourself?

How high is your self-esteem right now?

Is there anything about yourself that you would never want to change?

What do you love about yourself?

What do others love about you?

How can you love yourself even more?

Where are you going in life?

What is your personal best?

Have you found any video clips or movies about self-esteem, self-concept, and/or self-love that you especially enjoyed watching?

Life Lesson 3

Life Lesson 3

More Self-Exploration

When we feel safe and accepted, creativity flourishes. There are others in your life who might not enjoy your journey of self-discovery. Can you not listen to them? Be careful of self-doubt and those who like to encourage it. Appreciate the people:

- who enjoy how you problem solve and find your own solutions. We are each on our own unique path and what works for one person might not work for another.
- who truly appreciate and value your time, your life, and who you are.
- who ask for reasonable things in reasonable ways and at reasonable times.
- who do not need to be in control of everyone and everything.
- who are willing to admit mistakes rather than blame you when things go wrong.
- who truly care about others and are kind and considerate.
- who are helpful and dependable.

Spending time with positive people and away from negative people feeds your creative self. A creative life involves you lining up whenever possible to those feelings of hope and joy. Feed your imagination by truly paying attention to what would make you feel good. Keeping your attention on what feels good just plain feels good.

Let's take a short look at another interesting topic...anger. When anger comes to visit, it's a good idea to acknowledge it and then find some way to come to terms with it. Anger can be sneaky. It can grab you when you least expect it. However, when anger is erupting from inside, it's trying to get your attention. There's something in your life that is calling you. Anger can give you the impetus to move mountains, to forge ahead, and to find workable solutions that might have seemed unreasonable before. Anger gives us energy to move to a higher plane emotionally. How do we do that? We acknowledge its presence, see if there's an action we need to take, and then use that energy to ignite positive, rather than negative, feelings inside of ourselves. In other words, how can you make positively-charged lemonade from those angry lemons?

Anger helps us to solve situations that sometimes feel impossible to solve. Anger moves us on to new adventures. Do we need to wallow or dwell in the anger? Do we need to act it out? What we need to realize is that the anger is pointing us in a new and better direction—to a new and better solution. The creative self can help us to discover that solution and guide us to it.

What feels better to you: depression or anger? Anger usually does. It's a step up on the path to feeling better. Depression feels sad and lazy. It's sometimes hard to move, hard to function, hard to think, and hard to talk when we are depressed. Sometimes depression makes us feel ashamed. Anger can give us the energy to move and to act in our own best interests.

We can't avoid our heart's desires. If you try to, they will haunt you. Sometimes, when those dreams seem unattainable and impossible to reach, we let them sit on a shelf and we try to forget them. You can never forget your heart's desires. They will always tap you on the shoulder and try to get your attention. If you ignore your dreams and desires, they will keep coming back to remind you that they are waiting for fruition. By aligning yourself with the hope that they can be achieved, you will find the varied paths to achieving what you want.

Were you criticized and shamed as a youngster? Do you find it hard to allow yourself to keep moving forward because of it? Continual remembering of those events is like living it over and over again. The more you relive it, the worse you feel. The more you relive it, the more you keep it alive. Some choose to talk about the way they would have liked the past to have been instead. How can you keep filling your life with self-love—even with your memories? Let's say you are remembering feeling like a fool in fourth grade when the teacher caught you chewing gum. Perhaps she made you stand in front of the class with gum on your nose. The more you remember that, the more it brings up the old negative feelings. So now you want to take another class. You are an adult but the thought of school makes you immediately remember feeling like a fool in fourth grade. Just the thought of the classroom reminds you of this negative episode. You haven't let go of it yet. What can you do? How about speaking soothingly to yourself saying words like: I did the best I could when I was a child. If anything shameful happens in class, I am now an adult and

I can transfer to a different one. Wouldn't it be wonderful if this is the ideal class and the ideal teacher for me? Wouldn't it be great if the others in this class all became new friends? Isn't it going to be lovely when I learn so much more wonderful information on this subject? Aren't I going to enjoy meeting all these new folks and gathering new ideas on this topic? I can see that this time, school could begin to work out for me.

I know it sounds like a bit of a hokey example, but many times we hold on to past situations that we could be over and done with. It's time to move on to better opportunities in life. Thinking often about the past keeps us anchored in the past. It's time to look to better times in the future.

And what about criticism? Is it tough to deal with being criticized, even the constructive variety? If there's something useful in the criticism, keep those ideas. If it's malicious or hurtful, walk away. Isn't it also time to appreciate ourselves for our past endeavors rather than criticize ourselves because things didn't work out as well as we would have liked? It's time to accept our past and make way for the future. It's also time for more self-love, self-respect, and self-soothing. If the criticism reminds you of something from the past, find a way to accept that past situation. Then, it's time to envision a new and better scenario. Just because another person doesn't appreciate it, doesn't necessarily mean it's not worthwhile. In fact, even disasters can lead to greater things. Sometimes we need practice by making prototypes before we get it right. How many times might a pastry chef create a dessert before it's just the way he or she likes it and wants to serve it to others? Each not-so-perfect dessert points the way to a better one. It took Thomas Alva Edison over one thousand tries before the electric light bulb worked. That's a lot of prototypes! It's said that Edison didn't see them as failures and that they led the way to his being successful. Babe Ruth struck out 1,360 times in the Major Leagues plus thirty more times in World Series games. However, he had 714 home runs—more home runs than anyone else. How do you look at your strike outs? Are they opportunities for growth or do you consider them failures? I once heard that the Japanese symbol for problem is also the symbol for opportunity. With what attitude do you look at the contrast in your life?

Attitude is the key that can open many doors. Here's something fun to try. Find some time to relax and see how you can be just a little more creative each day. Increase your creativity by 1% and, oh my, in one hundred days, look what you've accomplished! Start telling yourself that you are getting more confident and motivated and less anxious. Then look for the evidence of it every day. You don't have to take huge leaps, just little steps.

Questions to Answer:

1. How many days this week did you write in your journal? How many pages did you write each time? Remember, if you are writing these pages, you are helping yourself. These pages are a weekly look at how you are feeling.

2. What did you do on your play date this week? On a scale of 1-10, how fun was your date?

3. Were you able to take fifteen minutes of complete and total relaxation just for you each day? How many days this week did you do that?

4. Have you been reading the supplementary book? Have you found anything that you especially liked, related to, or could use in your life right now? What have you discovered?

Please choose 8 out of the next 10 to answer:

5. Did anything happen this week that surprised or inspired you in a special way?

6. Is there an item from your childhood that you still treasure? If so, what is it and why?

7. What percent of the day is completely for you? 5%? 20%? 80%? How can you find more time just for you?

8. If you could have a new adventure right now, what would it be and why?

9. Write a story of compassion from your life. Who was compassionate to you and how did that affect you?

10. What do you enjoy doing that you haven't done in a long time? Name ten activities that you would like to have more time to incorporate into your life. If you've done them before, when was the last time you did them? When in the future might you be able to do any of these activities? It's nice to have something to look forward to, don't you think?

11. Is there anything you can change right now in your life that stands in your way of being more creative? What can you do about it? Is there another change you can make? Let's make it three—how about one more? Name the changes you will make.

12. What do you really think of creative people? Is there a creative person in the public eye who you truly admire?

13. Answer these quickly:

    A. I can

    B. I want

    C. My favorite present was

    D. I really appreciate

    E. A person I love unconditionally is

    F. Being creative is

    G. My idea of fun is

    H. A song that makes me feel good is

    I. I secretly love to

    J. The most beautiful place I ever saw was

    K. I really appreciate

    L. I am extremely confident when

14. Here are more to answer quickly:

    A. My closest friend likes

    B. The sport I enjoy the most is

    C. My favorite food is

    D. If I had more money I would

    E. My time is precious to me because

    F. I could really

    G. When I don't feel well, I like to

    H. I would believe in magic if

    I. The best compliment I ever received was

    J. Love is

    K. My favorite time of day is

    L. I like

       I like

       I like

       I like

       I really like

Questions for Discussion:

A. What is one of your dreams that you could see happening soon? Why is it important to you?

B. What is the best vacation you ever had and why? What kind of vacation would you like to go on next?

C. Where are you most comfortable? Describe it and how it feels to be there.

D. Who is your favorite movie or TV star? What is so wonderful about him or her?

Questions to Ponder:

What's the difference for you between destructive and constructive criticism?

How can you transform anger into a helping emotion?

When are you the most critical of yourself?

Why do you think that is?

When are you the least complimentary? Why?

When are you the most critical of others?

Why do you think that is?

When are you the most complimentary with others? Why?

How can you be even more self-supporting?

What films have you watched on compassion and/or anger management that were especially inspiring?

Life Lesson 4

Life Lesson 4

Vitality

Are you beginning to think about changes you would like to see happening within yourself? This often happens as you study intrapersonal communication or communication with self. The more we delve inside, the more self-aware we become. It can be very exciting to be on this road. Be diligent and you will reap many rewards. Just remind yourself whenever you can to enjoy the process.

Journaling allows you to be you. You don't have to put on a show or hide your true feelings. You get to write about whatever you want to write about. These are your thoughts—yours. No-one is looking over your shoulder and censoring you. In fact, you don't need anyone else to agree or disagree with you. What you write about are your thoughts and ideas—yours alone. This will make you stronger because you are getting to know your true self better. It's hard to lie to your journal. If someone at work is no longer acting like your friend or you feel frustrated or depressed or lonely, writing the true story in your journal can be transforming. You don't have to keep up any pretenses. You are telling your truth. You are opening a whole new section of your life—of you.

Sometimes we feel like skipping our journal writing. Try not to do that. The very time you feel like skipping the writing could be the time you need to write the most. Often it's when there are many feelings to process. Journaling is an especially good tool for this job. Are you angry at someone? Write it out! Put a big X through the pages when you are finished. Feel better? Usually you do.

Have you found that sometimes, when doing your journal writing, being too specific about touchy topics over and over again can feel uncomfortable? Have you also found that this reporting of the same negative situations ad infinitum makes you feel poor after a while?

When that starts to happen, it's time to turn a corner. I was once told that before you hit a brick wall you need to turn left. The more you self-explore, the easier it will be to turn left way before that wall. Does that mean you shouldn't vent in your journals? No. Vent as much as you need and want. If you find that you are repeating yourself and the venting is not feeling good anymore, then it's time to change tactics. A good soothing tactic is to get less detailed and write more generally about what is bothering you. See if that will make you feel better and give you more of a feeling of calm about the subject. Once you get to that place, it's time to experiment with looking at the other side of the coin.

I had the wonderful opportunity to once teach communication at the same college where the authors of my favorite textbook were teaching. I got to shake hands with Neil Towne and Ron Adler. For a communication professor, this is almost like meeting your favorite movie stars. I used their text in my classes for many years beginning with my first year of teaching. The text is called *Looking Out, Looking In.* They describe a pillow exercise from rural Japan in which children are taught to problem solve. They talk to one corner of a pillow and describe why they are right and those who disagreed with them are wrong. Then they talk to another corner of the pillow and describe why others who disagreed with them could be right and they could be wrong. I always thought that was a brilliant idea. To see the situation from the viewpoint of the other party makes one more compassionate and empathic. From one corner to the next, the problem solver has matured considerably. Then it's time to talk to the third corner by saying why both parties could be right and why both parties could be wrong. That's another really big step! When you feel like you can see both sides of the issue, you then tell the last corner of the pillow why the issue is not as important as it seems. Then there is still a bit more to do. Are you ready to finish the process and feel better because of it? The last thing to do is telling the middle of the pillow that there is truth to be seen from all sides of the issue.[1] Why not try this method? See if it brings you some answers and some relief when you need it.

Let's say you've written and written in your journal and it's all about the same issue over and over again. Perhaps it's time to change the channel. To get my mind off of a subject, I like to change the channel abruptly and write about something that is entirely different. Once the channel is changed and I've given myself a rest from the issue, many times, as I come back to rethink the old issue, a solution easily appears. Someone once told me that a change can be as good as a rest.

1. Adler and Towne, *Looking Out, Looking In*, 121, 123.

As you write in your journal you are starting to delete those old files that need to be deleted. Then you can make room for the new positive files that your creative self is ready to create. This can feel so good. Have you ever cleaned out an old closet and gotten rid of lots of outdated clothes you never wore? Then you realized you have so much room to fill it with new and wonderful clothes that you really like. You are cleaning out clutter from your life. Louise Hay was a brilliant speaker, counselor, author, and owner of one of the largest and most successful publishing houses worldwide. By the way, she decided to venture into publishing when she was in her late fifties. Louise also healed herself from cancer. She believed that whenever you clean away clutter, it's a good idea to repeat this positive affirmation: "I am cleaning out the closets of my mind."[2] So you are physically, emotionally, and spiritually giving yourself a thorough housecleaning. Isn't it wonderful to get rid of the old and then open your arms and make way for the new? Can you imagine how nice it feels to wipe the slate clean and begin anew? That's what you are doing! You are building your own vitality! It's time to get excited about letting the new you emerge!

It's also time to build more self-appreciation and joy. This week you might want to focus some of your journaling on appreciating what is around you—e.g. I'm so glad that I could sleep in this morning. Perhaps you want to affirm something you really want in your life—e.g. I trust that wonderful things are coming to me.

Are you having fun yet? It's time. Even when you do things that might not seem like fun, you can generate enough energy and enthusiasm to make them feel more fun. Looking on the sunny-side of the street gives you an energy that can't be beat.

I know that some days are more challenging than others to enjoy. However, the more you find those bits of joy throughout the day and the more you change the lemons into lemonade, the better life feels. How does life feel to you these days?

Have you ever had to do something you didn't want to do but you changed your attitude towards it? After the attitude changing, it wasn't really that bad, was it? I once had to have a shoulder operation. I didn't really want to do this but I decided to have a fun day anyway. I joked with the doctors and the nurses before the surgery and after. It eased my anxiety and the operation went smoothly. A positive attitude always trumps a negative one.

---

2. Hay, *You Can Heal Your Life*, 119.

You never know who you are going to meet and when you are going to meet them. I can't tell you how many times the right person turned up in the right place for me to make a major business connection in my life. However, if we are just living our lives unaware of the good that could be coming our way, we might miss the connections. As each idea comes to us, we must clear away our inner barriers to believing that it can happen for us.

Improbable events happen every day. The creative self can guide us to take actions when needed. Our job is to get ready to receive. Are you getting ready? How do you do that? There are times when I ask my creative self for answers and then I get involved in doing something else. Before long, the answers just seem to come to me when I least expect it. We are incredible beings with a wealth of knowledge and experience. We can do so much if we let our creative selves out to play.

Be careful of saying words to yourself like: it can never happen or I don't deserve it. Be careful of saying words to yourself like: it's too late, I'm too old (or not old enough), and it didn't happen before so why should it happen now. That's that negative voice telling the old, negative, I-don't-believe-it-can-happen-to-me story. Wonderful events take place every day. Just because something you wanted didn't happen yesterday doesn't mean that it can't happen today. Get ready for the good stuff! How do you do that? By appreciating what you have now. The more you appreciate, the more you can let in more to appreciate. The more you complain and worry and fret, the more you continue to complain and worry and fret. Do you want positive or negative results? Let's go for the positive. It's time to get ready to receive. The best way to receive something positive is to be optimistic. It's time to get a bit selfish and put your dreams, wants, and desires first.

Have you ever been jealous because another person has something you want? There's enough in life for everyone, you know. Just because someone else has the car I want doesn't mean there's not another one out there for me. Perhaps even a better one at a better price! Things often work out for us. Why shouldn't there be my ideal car on the horizon for me? Not enough cash? Ah—money comes to me in a variety of ways. Maybe I'll get a raise. Maybe I'll get a large tax refund. Maybe I'll inherit some funds. There are all kinds of roads to get what I want. It's time to get hopeful.

The more jealous we stay, the more we cement that jealousy into our existence. Do we want to keep being jealous or do we want to open our arms to receive the bounty we desire? Jealousy, like anger and resentment, blocks our creative juices from flowing. How can you feel better when you are jealous? What soothing words can you tell yourself? Can you envision yourself the receiver of all that you desire? Can you actually be happy for those who have received what you have been wanting in your life? Can you imagine even better for yourself? Has there ever been a situation where someone was jealous of something you had? What words would you say to him or her? Are you getting closer to letting go of the jealousy? Are you getting closer to believing that the good you desire can come to you? How close are you to being able to truly open yourself up for more of what you want?

Questions to Answer:

1. How many days this week did you write in your journal? How many pages each time? How is it going? How long does it take for you to start writing your most interesting stuff?

2. Did you do your play date this week? What did you do? How did it feel? On your fun meter from 1-10, rate your date.

3. Were you able to enjoy your daily quiet time this week? How many days? How much time?

4. This week choose a paragraph from your journal that you especially like and include it in this life lesson.

Please choose 8 out of the next 10 to answer:

5. Is there someone you are jealous of? Who is it and why? What new attitude is it possible for you to adapt that will soothe the jealousy and give you hope?

6. Pick a problem in your life and see if you can work this "pillow method" on it. Can you? Can you see all sides? Can you empathize with someone you disagree with? What's more important: being right or keeping peace in your communication? Are there times when it just doesn't matter who is right and who is wrong? Are there times you just want to agree to disagree? Are there times when the lines between right and wrong are not clearly defined? Are there times when there are two opposing voices inside you and you need to let them both vent? That's what journaling and this "pillow method" can help you to do.

7. How can you give yourself a break from something in order to let go of it? Make a list of some fun breaks (how about ten?) you can take to enable you to change the channel of your thoughts when you need to.

8. Name three activities you would like to transform from negative to positive? How will you do that?

9. What dream are you thinking is impossible? Is it truly impossible or is it just unlikely or improbable? Could you see part of it happening in the future?

10. Do you have strong enough faith to believe that dreams, your dreams, can come true? Do you have strong enough faith to allow yourself to dream about what you want? Do you have strong enough faith to allow yourself to accept what you want in life? If not, what can you do to change your attitude?

11. What are your three biggest strengths?

12. What do you consider your greatest weakness? How could you change that weakness into a strength?

13. Knowing what you don't want can help you see what you really do want. What would you really like in your life? Have fun completing the following:

I want

I want

I want

I want

I want

I want

I want

I want

I want

I want

14. Sometimes when I think of what I want, it reminds me that I don't have it yet. What brings me back into balance is thinking about what I have that I am most grateful for or what I so appreciate. What do you especially appreciate? Make a list of ten items and savor each one as you write. Can you list twenty?

Questions for Discussion:

A. What is your favorite holiday and why?

B. What is your favorite type of music? Why do you like to listen to it?

C. Does the weather affect you? Describe the weather for a perfect day in your life? What would be your second climate choice?

D. Are you happy where you live? If so, why? If not, what would you like more? Describe it.

Questions to Ponder:

How are you at problem solving?

Who is a good problem solver in your life?

What are your strengths and weaknesses?

How can you make your journal writing more fun?

What really stands in the way of your success?

Is there anything you can do about that?

What does vitality mean to you?

What gives you vitality? Why?

Has jealousy ever helped you to take a positive action?

Have you watched any video clips or movies about strength and vitality that you enjoyed?

Life Lesson 5

Life Lesson 5

Acceptance and Success

What are the best attitudes to have as you encourage yourself to be creative? How can you connect with your own inner creative self who so wants to express and be heard?

First of all, you need to be able to listen carefully to your very own self. The more you write, the more you relax, the more you quiet your thoughts, the more you allow yourself quality time on your play dates—the more you connect with the inner you. Through this connection, you become inspired. The inspiration gives you direction and tells you what to do next.

What if Michelangelo hadn't been inspired to sculpt *David*? I have traveled back to Florence just to see him yet again. Pictures don't do *David* justice. He is absolutely beautiful and standing near to him is one of the most awe-inspiring experiences of my life. Don't miss him! And to think, if Michelangelo hadn't listened to his own creative inspiration, the world might be lacking this great work of art.

With practice, we learn how to tune in to what the creative self is telling us. Once you accept the idea that it is natural and OK to create, you will start to hear that voice inside that gives you direction. Ever watch the old TV show *Magnum, P.I.?* I believe that was the first time that a character on a TV show—Magnum was played by Tom Selleck—listened to that little voice inside on a regular basis and admitted to it. At the time I thought it was interesting to watch a strong, male character listening to his intuitive voice. We women often joke about "women's intuition" and how we just seem to know what to do sometimes. Here was a male TV character telling the audience time and time again that that little voice inside—or his "male intuition"—had the right answers. That television show actually reinforced my self-listening skills.

Self-criticism and perfectionism can hold us back. It's bad enough to be put down by someone else, but being put down by your very own self is just not nice. How do you treat a loved one? How do you treat your best friend? How do you treat yourself? Have you complimented yourself lately? How much love and respect have you shown yourself? A little self-love and kindness goes a long way.

Trying to be perfect at first shot can block our abilities. It can block the creative warm-up work on our prototypes that's necessary for a project to breathe and expand. When I was a young girl, I visited the Metropolitan Museum of Art in New York City. I was lucky enough to be walking in back of a big tour group and heard the tour guide tell an interesting story about the Persian rugs on exhibit. These rugs were the size of large rooms and were hanging on the walls. They were the most beautiful rugs I had ever seen. Were they perfect? According to the tour guide, every rug had a mistake purposefully woven in because, according to the religion of the weavers, only Allah is perfect. Can you see the beauty in the imperfections of your life? Some would argue that there are no imperfections—that all is perfect as is. Can you open your heart to allow seemingly imperfect practice since it's in your practice where the seeds of greatness can be found? To start out expecting perfection on the first try can take you away from letting those seeds germinate. It's by moving, trying, and experimenting that we can produce the finished creation. We need time and thought to let the ingredients simmer together to become even better and better. It's usually more fun when the pressure is off. The more fun it is, the more we want to continue. Acceptance is the key. When I allow my dreams, goals, and desires, I get led step-by-step on the yellow brick road of my own life. Life gives me the guide posts to follow when I am connected to my own creative self. That connection is vital. Let's let the creative self out to play. What a party we can have!

Success comes in many sizes and shapes. Notice and appreciate the smallest achievement. The more we celebrate our successes, the more success will come. Appreciate, enjoy, celebrate—how can it get any better? We can believe so much in our own abilities that we begin to appreciate, enjoy, and celebrate before we are even finished. Can you generate those feelings without the end result? Sure you can. Do it often and you will enjoy every minute more.

Success in most countries is measured by the Gross National Product. The fourth dragon king of the country of Bhutan, Jigme Singye Wangchuck, believed that success in his country should be measured by the peace and happiness of the people—not by how much they own. He felt that the Gross National Happiness is a better indicator of success.[3] What about you?

3. Wangchuck, quoted in "Gross National Happiness."

Questions to Answer:

1. How many days this week did you write in your journal? How many pages did you write each day? Are you allowing yourself to appreciate this ritual yet?

2. How was your play date? What did you do and how much did you enjoy it? Where did it fall on the 1-10 fun scale?

3. Were you able to take fifteen minutes of complete and total relaxation just for you each day? How many days this week did you do that?

4. Did anything happen this week that surprised or inspired you in a special way?

Please choose 8 out of the next 10 to answer:

5. Who is the most self-accepting person you know? What is he/she like?

6. How can you be happier today? Name five things that you can do that will make you more joyful.

7. If you rubbed the magic lamp and a genie appeared right now to give you any three wishes, what would you chose *right now* and in what order of importance would they fall? Are your dreams changing or staying the same? Why or why not?

8. How would it feel to have one of those wishes right now? Can you feel it? Describe that feeling. Do that for the other two wishes. Describe how having each would feel. Could you feel those feelings even when your dreams haven't happened yet?

9. How happy are you? Does the more you accumulate make you happier? Why or why not? Would you agree with the ruler of Bhutan?

10. What is a part of your life that you didn't appreciate and now you do? Describe it. What happened?

11. Name and describe five fun ways to celebrate success.

12. Your creative self wants to give you an award. What would it be for and why?

13. Write a short acceptance speech for this award.

14. Have you envisioned any obstacles that stand in the way of your success? What are they? Name the top five. How can you look at each of these problems as opportunities?

Questions for Discussion:

A. What is your ideal of the perfect family?

B. What is your favorite sport? Why do you like it so much?

C. What is your favorite outfit to wear? What do you like so much about it?

D. How easy is it for you to take care of yourself in difficult situations?

Questions to Ponder:

What are some successes that you have every day?

How do you reward yourself when you are successful?

What is your favorite compliment?

Are you becoming your own best friend?

Are there any negative influences in your life that you no longer appreciate?

Is there anything you can do about that?

Do you value your own creative energy?

Who is the most creative person you know?

Have you ever hurt yourself emotionally with perfectionism?

What are you creating—cooking up—in your life right now?

Have you watched any films about success lately?

Life Lesson 6

Life Lesson 6

Imagination, Enthusiasm, Hope

Children are great dreamers. They know how to use their imaginations well. Adults leading busy lives sometimes feel like those days are gone forever. The good news is that we can regenerate our ability to imagine anytime we want to. It just takes a little enthusiasm, desire, and energy. It doesn't have to be erased entirely from our lives just because we are now grown-ups.

As your imagination encourages you to build positive scenarios by creative visualizing, your imagination can also build negative scenarios by worrying. Worry and you get more to worry about. That paints a negative future. That doesn't feel so good, does it? Creatively visualize and you paint a positive picture of the future. What picture do you want to paint? One feels good and the other one doesn't. I like to go with the one that feels good, don't you?

I sometimes get nervous driving in unfamiliar territory. One thing I like to do to make the drive easier is to see myself—before I go—driving smoothly and getting the best parking spot easily. Before I leave I like to take some time appreciating my car and imagining a lovely drive. It's just a little tweaking to see the glass half-full rather than half-empty. It always makes the drive more fun.

Isn't it lovely to be encouraged? Encouragement makes us feel good and helps us to achieve. Add in some support and understanding and the creative self soars. It's wonderful to get this from other people, but how nice to be able to give this to ourselves.

This type of adventure is different from many others in a typical community. What we are trying to achieve here is something more unique. Many of us were shamed early on in our creative endeavors because we could not conform to the rules made by others. We do need to keep growing and this adventure is an avenue to do that. These ideas have been successful time and time again. I hope you are enjoying the process.

When we feel hopeful, so much seems possible. Hope gives us a fresh perspective—a feeling of possibility. Did you know that you can generate a feeling of hope even when you aren't feeling that way? We can also generate enthusiasm whenever we choose. It's your choice. Enthusiasm gives us energy to accomplish.

Enthusiasm also helps us to create. Enthusiasm can be created even when you don't think it can be. I like to generate enthusiasm on a daily basis—some days more than others. I often wake up enthusiastic and ready to go. If I don't, I can create that feeling. I have to get into an attitude of play to do this. If work feels like play, I do it better. Life feels better to me that way. What about you?

Some emotions feel great and others don't. Remember, when you feel good, your creative juices flow. When you feel good, life feels easy and fun. When you feel good, the world looks rosier. Making the jump from not feeling good to feeling better can take some creativity. Look for ways to make yourself feel incrementally better and better and you will. Making the jump from being depressed to feeling ecstatically joyful is a pretty tough thing to do. Feel the feelings as you keep moving through them going from negative to positive. Pretty soon life can feel more hopeful and better again, don't you think? Feeling hopeful can open the door to even more happier feelings. We can always generate a feeling of hopefulness, if we let ourselves. Your creative self can show you, if you let it. After a while, dealing with feelings becomes easier and more fun to do. Feeling better is always the goal.

Every end is a new beginning. Hope is the key. There's always something around the corner. If you stay home complaining about what you don't have, you miss the other side of the coin—what you could have. Keep dreaming. Keep thinking of the future. Keep knowing that there are lots of great opportunities along the way. But you won't find them if you are complaining about not having enough great opportunities. Life is a process, an adventure. Get ready to dig in. Ever see that movie *What about Bob*? Taking baby steps is important.

We feel empowered when we feel good.

We feel empowered when we take care of ourselves.

We feel empowered when we put ourselves first.

We feel empowered when we enjoy our lives.

We feel empowered when we appreciate ourselves.

We feel empowered when we strive to become our personal best.

What makes you feel good? What gives you hope? How else can you feel your own personal power?

Questions to Answer:

1. How many days this week did you write in your journal? How many pages? Have you allowed yourself to daydream even more than usual?

2. Did you take your play date this week? What did you do? How did it feel? Were you able to take more than one this week? How fun was it on the 1-10 fun scale? What are you thinking of doing for a play date next week?

3. Were you able to take fifteen minutes of complete and total relaxation just for you each day? How many days this week did you do that?

4. Have you found any concepts in the supplementary book that you especially liked, related to, or could use in your life right now? Describe them.

Please choose 8 out of the next 10 to answer:

5. A lack of imagination in my life encourages:

   Using my imagination makes me feel:

   What's so great about using your imagination?

6. How do you think that imagination has served the world historically, culturally, and personally? Please give an example of each.

7. What are you hopeful about right now?

8. What are you not hopeful about but wish you were? How can you generate hope and enthusiasm for it?

9. How do you generate enthusiasm for something you aren't that thrilled about? Write out an example of a time when you did this.

10. How much of your day are you generating positive feelings? 10%? 40%? 75%? 90%? How can you generate even more?

11. How have you gone from feeling lousy to feeling good lately? How long did it take? How could it have taken a shorter time?

12. Describe an ideal weekend. Where would you go and what would you do?

13. List five fun things that you can incorporate into your daily life this week. They don't have to be big time consumers. For example, you could listen to music while you brush your teeth.

14. Describe one of your fondest memories.

Questions for Discussion:

A. Describe another favorite memory. What happened? Why was it so wonderful?

B. What are you planning to do for yourself this week that will make you feel good?

C. If you could change anything in your life right now, what would it be and how would you like to do it?

D. Describe a recent "aha" moment in your life.

Questions to Ponder:

How have you been using your imagination lately?

What delightful scenarios have you been cooking up for yourself?

How enthusiastic are you on a daily basis?

Does anger or frustration over not having what you want ever get in your way when imagining?

What can you do about that?

How do you like to clear your mind?

How can you creatively visualize more often?

How does one build more confidence?

What is your favorite relaxation method?

What do you most appreciate in your daily life?

Have you watched any video clips or movies that have inspired your imagination or given you a feeling of hope?

Life Lesson 7

Life Lesson 7

Self-Trust and Future Goals

John Glenn was the first man to orbit the earth. He used to hum when things got tough. He hummed "The Battle Hymn of the Republic" when he re-entered the atmosphere. This was at a time when he wasn't absolutely certain his space capsule would make it. Humming was his friend. It gave him solace. If you love to sing and to listen to music, do it more often, especially when you are busy. It might make you feel like you are taking time out for yourself even though you might not be.

Someone once told me that fear is two-faced: it's a bully—but if you look it in the eyes, it becomes a coward and runs away. Just because you find it hard to begin a project, it doesn't mean you will not be able to do it. Sometimes it is fear that stands in the way. If I'm scared about doing something, it often means that I'm not ready. Sometimes it's because I'm trying to do too much all at once. Some people say that the cure for fear is love and that the opposite of fear is faith. Taking baby steps on a project is the beginning of walking through the fear and can be considered an act of love. Self-love. Waiting until you are connected with your creative self and are open to listening as that intuitive voice guides you is an act of love. Trying to force or punish yourself into starting a project would be the opposite. Beginning something when you are inspired feels too good. Don't miss out!

If I have mixed feelings about an action I'm about to take, it can mean that it's not the right time for me to take the action. I used to go by the idea that if 51% of me wants to do something, then I should do it. Now I try for a higher percentage. One way to get clearer about decisions is through deep relaxation because it helps to clear your mind while completely relaxing your body. With a clear mind, making decisions becomes easier. Giving yourself quiet time is a wonderful way to connect with your inner creative self and let the worries of the day fall off your shoulders. It's like taking a mini-vacation. There are many successful relaxation methods on the market. You could pick one that speaks to you. Some like to use guided relaxations so all they have to do is listen and off they go. Others concentrate on a repetitive word or phrase or watch a candle light flicker. Some take power naps. Some tense and release different body parts in order to squeeze out tension and relax more. Others meditate. Some believe in relaxing for fifteen minutes a day and others believe in forty minutes twice a day. Again, pick the method and the time that works for you. I have a friend who has been enjoying his relaxation periods twice a day for forty minutes each time for forty years. He seems to always be cool, calm, and clear. Thomas Alva Edison used to nap every day to clear his mind and look at all he invented. How can you take a break from the chattering inside?

Some believe that doing exercise before relaxing brings you to a deeper level. Some also believe that full, deep, diaphragmatic breathing will encourage deeper levels, too. The deeper we can breathe, the more fully we can relax. The breath is a natural tonic for calming down. Feeling nervous, upset, or angry? Try taking ten full deep breaths. Afterwards you might still be nervous, upset, or angry, but I bet you will be less so, perhaps even much less so.

Deep relaxation can benefit us physically, emotionally, and spiritually. It's been said to lower blood pressure, to calm our nerves, to reduce anxiety, to control nervousness, to relax us, to enhance our immune systems, and to help us control pain levels. It can help us deal with emotions, to sleep better and deeper and to need less sleep, to increase our desire and ability to create, and to be more tolerant. When deeply relaxing, we get closer to our own inner, creative selves. It gives us a feeling of connectedness. After a period of quiet time I often have answers and solutions I didn't have before. It seems to sort me out and helps me to be my own best friend. It helps me to rely on myself. Going within for peace and reflection can help me to hear the answers, ideas, and solutions that have been simmering inside. This practice allows me to deeply connect with myself. It's been well worth the time.

A great time to deeply relax is before we go to sleep. Because it clears the mind and feels so good, many times we wake up in a wonderful mood as a result. Some find it easier to fall asleep because they are so peaceful. Another great time for this practice is first thing in the morning and, if we have relaxed well before sleeping, another period of relaxation will continue that great mood. If you are coming out of a time of relaxation feeling sad or unhappy, it could mean that it's time to come to a peaceful way of thinking about what is bothering you. Say soothing phrases to yourself that you believe such as, "life can be good when I look for the good." Remember examples of times when things worked out for you. Or switch your attention and think about something else entirely. Appreciating your family, friends, or your job might be good thoughts to switch to. I've been told that appreciation can be just as powerful as deep relaxation. So, if you don't enjoy getting deeply relaxed, try a round or two of appreciation.

The more you appreciate, the better you feel. Even in the midst of something unpleasant, it is still possible to be appreciative. In fact, the feeling of appreciation can bring you more to appreciate in your life. Make a list of ten positive aspects of yourself or your life each day to build self-appreciation. Aim for twenty or thirty whenever you can. I know people who do this every day and they feel so good. Or think of one positive aspect of yourself on the first day. Think of two on the second day. Keep increasing your list until you get to one hundred. By that time, I bet you will be feeling a lot of self-appreciation.

I rarely wake up in a bad mood these days because I spend so much time appreciating myself. If I do wake up feeling poor, the first thing I would do is begin appreciating. I have a friend who is a brilliant appreciator. He starts in the morning as soon as he wakes up. He begins his day by appreciating his pillow, his bed, his sheets and blankets, his room, his home, his stuff, etc. As he turns on the light switch he appreciates having electricity. As he turns on the faucet, he becomes grateful he doesn't have to walk miles to fill up a bucket from the river. In some countries, people still have to do that. What are you appreciating? Remember, that feeling can be contagious. Isn't it more fun to hang around with yourself when you feel happy about life and appreciative of all you have? The next time someone begins to get on your nerves, try looking for something—anything—to appreciate about him or her. When I do this, I find that it switches my attention. Then, all of a sudden, he or she isn't as annoying. The more we look for things to appreciate, the more we find to appreciate. There's so much to love in the world. Look at the sky, the mountains, the lakes, the rivers, the ocean, the beaches, the birds, the people, the stores, the architecture, the cars, the homes...I could go on forever. What or who are you appreciating right now?

There are times when we stand in our own way. We come so far and then we think that we can't go on. Sometimes we hide. Sometimes we get sick or injured to avoid the next step. Have you ever done that? We don't have to. The more we appreciate ourselves and have faith in our own decisions, the easier and better our lives become. Sometimes we make a decision and just go with whatever choice feels best at the time. Rather than second guess, trust yourself. You know what is best for you. There are others who would like us to do it their way. Until they have walked in our shoes and lived our lives, how can they truly know what is good for us?

OK, let's get cooking. You are getting in touch with your creative selves. Some of you are endeavoring to create what you want to create for yourselves. From the first minute I taught a college communication class in 1975, I knew what I wanted to create in my own life. I wanted to be a college communication professor forever. I knew in my heart of hearts that it was what I had been born to do. Unfortunately, I was told repeatedly that finding full-time work in my field would be extremely tough. The field was overflowing and there were very few full-time opportunities to be had. However, I always had plenty of part-time work during my first decade of teaching. Every semester I looked forward to my classes and to meeting all of my new students. They were some of the best years of my teaching career and I felt blessed to have had so much wonderful work.

Others in my life weren't very happy that even though I was doing what I loved to do, I wasn't making a lot of money—very, very little, in fact. They wanted me to use my intelligence and talents in an arena where I would be paid more money. I wasn't thrilled about doing that, but, after six years of doing what I loved to do, I decided to give in to all the pressure and take a more prosperous and secure job as a Training Specialist at the World Trade Center in New York City. From college teaching to the corporate world was a big jump for me and there was much to appreciate at my new job. For the first month I was asked to read all of the books in the corporate library. Since I love reading, that was a good start. One book encouraged readers to dream about life and to list goals for the future. That dreaming gave me such insight. It pointed the way and helped me to get clear about my future aspirations. My heart's desire was to find a way back to the classroom. I also knew that I wanted to relocate to a warmer climate, near the beach. It was about two years later that I was back to college teaching, but this time in sunny, Southern California. Now that made me very happy! It wasn't long after that that I was hired as a full-time teacher.

My experience at the World Trade Center gave me the impetus to change my life. It taught me so much about myself and listening to my own inner guidance. I periodically ask myself if I'm still following my heart's desires and, if I'm not, I know it's time to make some changes to do so. What about you?

Questions to Answer:

1. How was your journal writing this week? Did you write three times on three different days? Were you tempted to take a break from writing or is it becoming more of an integral part of your life these days?

2. How was your play date? Even if you can't find a few hours to play, do try to find some time just for you. It really helps to handle stress and can make you happy. If life is really busy, try dividing the play date into half-hour intervals on different days. Coming back from a half-hour play date can be very refreshing, depending on what you did. On the fun scale of 1-10, how was your play date this week? What did you do?

3. Were you able to take fifteen minutes of complete and total relaxation just for you each day? How many days this week did you do that?

4. Who and/or what in your life makes you feel safe? Why?

Please choose 8 out of the next 10 to answer:

5. Make believe that you have just had your eighty-fifth birthday and you are reminiscing with friends and family. What would you wish you had accomplished in your life?

6. What do you see yourself doing for the next few years? What would you really like to do?

7. If you could take a year off, how would you spend that year? What would be your top priority? What would you do?

8. If you knew that you didn't have very long to live, what would you do with the rest of your life?

9. Is there anyone in your life who would resent you having your dreams come true? Is there anything you can appreciate about that person?

10. How much do you trust yourself? When? Why?

11. What is something nice that has happened to you recently? How did it make you feel?

12. Is there a goal that you are especially concerned about? Are there any baby steps that you can take to begin your walk of faith?

13. List your future goals. What do you want to accomplish?

14. It's time to remember that sometimes how we figure out what to do next is by experimenting. Our so-called mistakes and failures are often the turning points in our lives. How has something you thought was a mistake or a failure led you on to something even better? In other words, describe a time where you made lemons into lemonade.

Questions for Discussion:

A. Who is a role model for you? Why?

B. What have you done lately that is lots of fun?

C. Who is one of your creative goals for today?

D. If you could invent a reality show for you to be on, what would it be like?

Questions to Ponder:

Have you ever stood in your own way?

What happened?

When are times that you might second-guess yourself?

Who is someone in your life who appreciates you?

Who do you especially appreciate?

What future plans do you have that you have put on hold?

When will you start working on them again?

How much do you trust yourself to make the best decisions in life?

What will it take to develop more self-trust?

When do you feel most encouraged?

Have you watched any films that encouraged self-trust?

Life Lesson 8

Life Lesson 8

Dreaming

Building daydreams is a wonderful thing to do but only when these daydreams feel good. If thinking about what you would love in life makes you feel sad because you don't already have what you want, then it's time to switch to another fantasy. So, when is daydreaming wonderful? When it makes you feel good. When it doesn't feel good, you can always switch those thoughts and pursue another dream. As Eric Butterworth used to say each morning on his New York radio show back in the 1970's, "You can change your life by altering your thoughts." What thoughts are you thinking? The happier your thoughts, the happier you will be. When something doesn't feel good, it's your job to find a way to soothe your spirit.

So, how do you soothe yourself about a dream that hasn't come true yet and which you might doubt will ever come true? Each of us has our own individual ways to do that. What if your dream is to buy a new house, but right now you don't have the funds for it. If every time you think of the house of your dreams you feel sad that it's not in your life yet, then you need to find a way to just push it onto the "back burner" so that your dream can one day come to reality. Dreaming about something that you have doubts will happen doesn't feel good and that can keep you from taking the actions you need to pursue your dream.

Rather than dream about the home, you could dream about something else that you believe is easily attainable. That produces a feeling of hope and excitement. If, however, the thought of not having that home keeps coming into your consciousness and won't leave you alone, it's time to figure out a way to positively think about that dream home. How about just thinking generally about how this dream might not be a possibility now, but it could be a possibility in the near future. Is that a better thought for you? Do you know of anyone who had been in your situation and had eventually found themselves a nicer home? That would be a good story to revisit.

And what about the idea that things in life often go our way. There are jewels in the rough. There are deals to be had. Thinking positively helps us to believe in the possibility. What about where you live now? Is there anything you love and appreciate about where you now live? Even if it's not your ideal place, appreciating your home and noticing what is so good about it will make you more conscious of what you want in your future home. It will also make your daily living more enjoyable. Just because you notice and appreciate where you are now living does not mean that you have to stay there forever. You might find that all that appreciation makes you enjoy your present domicile more. That's not a bad thing. It feels good to enjoy. You don't have to hate a home to move to another one. The more you appreciate your home, the better you feel. The better you feel, the more you attract better-feeling things into your life.

How do you feel happy in the middle of an unhappy thought? You usually don't. However, just like in the above example, you can come to terms with that negative thought by taking the focus off of the details. Then go do something else, if you can. A positive action can take away a negative thought. If the negative thought keeps coming back, soothe yourself so you aren't thinking about what you don't have. The idea is to enjoy your present circumstances as much as you can. The more you appreciate what you have, the better you will feel about life. The better you feel about life, the better life is. The better life is for you, the happier you are.

I once heard a story about a famous Hollywood personality. I heard that when he was starting out he would park his car daily so that he could stare at the Hollywood sign while he envisioned himself living the prosperous life of a successful actor. He also wrote himself a check for ten million dollars and put it under his pillow. Every night before he went to sleep and every morning when he woke up, he visualized himself earning that much money from acting. Take a guess at how much money he supposedly made for his first movie? Ten million dollars! Was it coincidence, voodoo, just plain luck, or self-fulfilling prophecy? Would you say that he used the power of his imagination and positive attitude to attract that into his life?

What about your dreams? How would it feel to have them come true right now? Can you imagine that feeling and feel it anyway before the dream comes true? You can feel good even when everything you want isn't in your life. That's the idea. The better you feel, the more you can allow even more wonderful events to take place. How good do you want to feel? How many great feelings can you handle? Open up your heart to allow yourself to feel good no matter what. Very often you can change a negative to a positive just by your attitude towards it. How often are you making lemonade out of the lemons? The quicker you do that, the better life feels. Dwelling on the discomfort of the problem, keeps it alive and active in your life. Again, how good do you want to feel? Then let go of whatever doesn't feel good and switch to a better-feeling, positive channel in your mind.

Questions to Answer:

1. Did you journal three times a week on three different days? Did you feel like writing more often than that? Were you able to spend more time journaling about positive ideas than negative ones?

2. How was your play date? What did you do? On a fun scale of 1-10, please rate this date.

3. Were you able to take fifteen minutes of complete and total relaxation just for you each day? How many days this week did you do that?

4. Are you enjoying reading the supplementary book? Are there any new ideas that you related to?

Please choose 8 out of the next 10 to answer:

5. Is there anything that is new and exciting in your life?

6. Why do you deserve the best for yourself?

7. In an ideal world, how soon would you like your dreams to happen? Are you really ready for them? What could you do to be even more ready?

8. How often do you allow yourself to daydream? Does daydreaming generate positive or negative feelings? What do you like to daydream about?

9. Does this all seem like pie-in-the-sky thinking or are you actually seeing evidence in your life of the benefits of thinking positively?

10. How many others know about your dreams? Is that helpful to you? Are there any dreams that you tossed aside because of someone else's advice? How did that work out for you?

11. Have you felt especially inspired lately to take any dream-related actions? Does taking an action feel light and right? Or does it feel heavy and full of questions?

12. What is an activity that always makes you feel good? How often can you do it?

13. When in your life did one of your wishes come true? What happened and how did it feel?

14. What is your favorite way of celebrating? Would you be willing to celebrate now in the expectation of wishes being fulfilled?

Questions for Discussion:

A. What success from the past would you like to remember?

B. What song really gets you going and why?

C. What is something positive that you are looking forward to right now?

D. What is your individual style? Describe yourself.

Questions to Ponder:

Who told you that dreams can't come true?

What wonderful dreams have come true for you?

Who or what stands in the way of you getting more of what you want?

Do you have a vivid imagination?

How can you make it even more vivid?

How will you feel when your most cherished dreams come true?

Can you feel those feelings even when the dreams aren't fulfilled yet?

How will you celebrate when your desires are fulfilled?

Who in your life believes in you the most?

Why?

Are you ready to watch a video about dreams coming true?

An Introduction to the Video: *Dreams Can Come True*

Have many dreams come true for you? For those whose dreams do come true, it seems they really believed it was possible and/or their desire was so strong, the outcome simply couldn't be otherwise. So, if you believe that something good is right around the corner, it probably is. In fact, sometimes what you receive is better than what you originally hoped for or imagined.

Occasionally, what you want just turns up at your door step. Now and then, you just know that it's important to take an action which leads to getting what you want. Sometimes it feels like what you want is very far away, and then again, you might feel it's so close that you can touch it. If thinking about your most cherished dream makes you feel sad because you don't have it fulfilled already, a good strategy is to switch to any other thought that feels better to think about. The idea is to feel good in your life. Feeling good just seems to generate more and more good-feeling thoughts and ideas. Pretty soon, you'll be seeing more good-feeling people and opportunities come into your life. Then things continue to get better all the way around.

The video called *Dreams Can Come True* was made especially for you. These are stories of others whose dreams have come true plus a guided dream relaxation for you to enjoy. I, personally, love hearing how dreams have come true for others because it motivates me to believe in my own dreams. Stories like these give me hope and faith that my dreams can come true, too. I'm reminded that so much is possible in life. Often, what I have dreamed about hasn't happened yet, but then something more wonderful than I could have ever imagined occurs in my life. If I'm not thinking positively I can sometimes miss those wonders. I'm hoping that these stories and this dream relaxation will give you a jump-start to hoping and believing your dreams can come true, too. Please visit www.learnquickly.com/creativeself.htm if you would like more information.

I think the video works best divided into three parts. Begin with the first three stories from **Jake**, **Joy**, and **David**. After you read Life Lesson 9, continue with the next three stories from **Mellissa**, **Dan**, and **Laura**. After you read Life Lesson 10, continue with the last two stories from **Jeff** and **Sherry**. Then enjoy *A Dream Relaxation* from **David**.

The more you believe, the more things happen for you. What are you thinking about these days? What are you believing? Just because one of your dreams hasn't quite happened yet, that doesn't mean that another one can't happen for you. Isn't there a magic to believing? Remember: if you really think that good things are right around the corner for you, then they probably are. Keep looking around the corner in anticipation and see what can happen for you!

Life Lesson 9

Life Lesson 9

Abundance

Is there something that stands in the way of you being able to create what you want for yourself? Can you let go of this hindrance? Is it fear? The opposite is faith. Do try seeing what you want and focusing on your dream. If when you do that, it makes you sad in any way, then pick something to think about that feels better without any negativity attached.

I usually can think about animals without any negativity at all. What about you? Are there any topics you can think about that have absolutely no past, present, or possible future negativity attached? If I think about a dream and feel like it's never going to come, it will probably never come. That's that self-fulfilling prophecy idea. So it's better that I change what I'm dreaming about and think about something that doesn't have any negativity attached to it. What are the positive parts of your life? Let's choose those thoughts instead. The more we think positively, the better we feel. The better we feel, the more we notice other wonderful events around us. The more we notice, the more appear!

Choosing thoughts that feel best is not always the easiest thing to do. However, those "best" thoughts can make you feel so good! Scientists say that we think about 70,000 thoughts a day. Rather than trying to control them, how about just trying to think thoughts that make you feel good? Feeling good and having fun is such a wonderful part of life, don't you think? Sometimes in the hustle and bustle we forget those simple truths. You choose what to give your attention to. You can choose how you feel. You can also make a choice about what you would like to dream about. Keep thinking about what it will feel like when you have accomplished what you want to accomplish. Keep enjoying and appreciating every minute you have. Keep being hopeful that the good is coming now. It can come to you if you expect it. (Just remember, if you are expecting the bad, it can multiply, too.) What do you want? Don't worry about where it will come from. If you can make the best of everything and trust in what tomorrow will bring, life will get better and better.

I was brought up to believe that only the privileged minority get to have the lives they want. It was difficult for me to believe that I could have a life where I could do the work I love to do. Who is going to pay us to do what we love to do? Are we going to get paid to sing, dance, speak, act, write, cook, bake, design homes, sculpt, paint, surf, ski, swim, play music, write songs, etc. just because we like to do these things? I was told that those kinds of activities were for hobbies, not for jobs. Who was I to think that I deserved to do what I wanted to do? Who was I to believe that I could achieve what I wanted when many didn't?

But these criticisms finally led me to ask myself, "Why do I think that?" I am a uniquely talented person who has already seen many of my dreams come true. I refuse to believe that the rest of my dreams won't come true. I now know that it's only a matter of me getting ready to receive them. Are you ready for yours to come true?

When I am in the flow of life, doors seem to open for me wherever I go. Marvelous things appear. Wonderful events just happen. When I feel deserving and worthy, everything comes my way. I meet the right people at the right times. The right connections come through. I feel important and useful. Work isn't work—it's play and it's fun. And money seems to flow right to me.

A long time ago, I used to say often that I never won anything. Then someone said to me that if I keep saying that, I'll continue to never win anything. It's that self-fulfilling prophecy idea. So one day many years ago, I walked into a beautiful store in the Hillcrest area of San Diego. They were having a raffle on an Easter basket full of their beautiful hand-made goodies. It was a basket worth a hundred dollars and many years ago, that was a big deal. So, I took a chance thinking that I could possibly be a winner. It was certainly a possibility. Guess what? I won! After that I could no longer say I never won anything. I continued to win and win whenever I joined in a raffle. I had discovered my own winning attitude!

I've heard many teachers over the years talk in the same vein about abundance and prosperity. We can feel rich in so many different ways not necessarily having to do with money. In what ways are you rich today? According to the famous author, publisher, and speaker Louise Hay, being abundant is not just about money. You could be abundant in time, abundant in love, abundant in food, abundant in talent, abundant in health, abundant in happiness, abundant in family and friends, abundant in vacation plans—you get the idea?[4] I used to ask my classes each day if they had become any richer. At first they thought I was a bit strange. Then they caught on. One of my students was very young and came from an extremely dysfunctional family system. He was in a recovery program and had struggled with depression. It took some time for him to start seeing the positive side of this exercise. Then one day he responded by saying that the night before he went for a swim in the ocean in the rain. He said he felt sleek like a seal and he felt richer for the experience. It felt like swimming in velvet and he felt decadent for the opportunity. Another student, who had been fighting on and off with her husband all week, said that she had had the most wonderful candlelight dinner with him the night before. Harmony had been restored. Another student had received a completely unexpected check in the mail. How rich do you want to feel? How can you let those feelings into your life?

Pampering is a fun tool. It's good to treat ourselves well and we don't have to go into debt to do that. A new pair of socks can be a treat. Eating a sweet, juicy mango on a hot, sunny day brings joy to my heart. A long bubble bath with candles flickering and beautiful background music can soothe your spirit. The better you feel, the more abundant you feel. The more abundant you feel, the more abundance you let in. How abundant do you want your life to be? How much more can you envision for yourself? How much more can you give yourself? How much more pampered do you want to be?

Let's face it, money is a relatively recent phenomenon. It's just a way to barter. But we all have such interesting beliefs about money. I would be willing to bet you already know what life truly means and how lucky you are no matter how much money you have. After all, money is just paper that represents degrees of wealth—but that paper is often loaded with feelings. What kinds of positive feelings do you want to feel about money, wealth, and prosperity? Have you ever heard of *Pollyanna?* She liked to play the "glad game" where she saw the positive side of a negative situation—looking at the glass half-full rather than half-empty. It really works and makes life a lot more fun.

According to Jerry and Esther Hicks in their best-selling book, *Ask and it is Given*, we are told that, "You have to feel good about great abundance before you will allow the pleasure of great abundance to flow into your experience."[5] So we can all be more prosperous by just feeling positive about being prosperous. The more prosperous we feel, the more prosperity comes to us! Feelings are like magnets!

4. Hay, *Receiving Prosperity*, compact disc.
5. Hicks and Hicks, *Ask and it is Given*, 248.

Questions to Answer:

1. How did you enjoy writing in your journal this week? Did you write three pages on three different days?

2. How was your play date this week? What did you do? On a scale of 1-10, how much fun did you have doing it?

3. Were you able to take fifteen minutes of complete and total relaxation just for you each day? How many days this week did you do that?

4. As you are writing your journal pages, mark off a paragraph that you would like to include as the answer to this question.

Please choose 8 out of the next 10 to answer:

5. Make a list of ten ways that you can easily and affordably pamper yourself. How soon can you do these things? Put a possible date next to each.

6. Put the list somewhere special to remind you that you deserve to feel good. Where did you put it?

7. What were you taught to think about prosperity and abundance? Do those ideas still resonate with you? Why or why not?

8. Are there any non-supportive people in your life who are hindering your creativity and are standing in the way of your communication with yourself? How much time do you spend with them? Are you able to spend less time with them? Why or why not?

9. For this exercise, find some kind of a container like a box, a bag, a bowl, or a jar. This will be your special dream container. Every time you see a picture of something you have been dreaming about, cut it out and put it in the container. Keep choosing dreams and thoughts that you enjoy. Remember, dreams can change over time. Just because you've gotten what you wanted doesn't mean there isn't more for you out there! Where did you put it? What does it look like?

10. Who is someone who truly inspires you? Why?

11. If you had $50,000 to spend in the next hour, what would you buy?

12. Would having more money in your life make you happier? What would it feel like to have lots and lots of money?

13. What is a rags-to-riches story that has inspired you and your beliefs?

14. What does abundance feel like to you? How can you generate more of that feeling in your life?

Questions for Discussion:

A. You are going to be stranded for a few weeks on a desert island and you can bring three “luxury” items with you. What would they be?

B. Name and explain one quality about you that you especially appreciate.

C. How much money would you really like to have?

D. If you just won one million dollars, what is the first thing you would buy? Why? What would you do with the rest of the money?

Questions to Ponder:

How are you appreciating yourself more and more each day?

What else are you appreciating in your life?

How abundant do you really want to be?

How much do you allow yourself to dream?

What kinds of positive feelings do you have towards prosperity?

How often throughout the day do you feel abundant?

How much more abundant could you feel?

How would you do that?

What fun surprises have come your way lately?

Are you ready to watch the next three stories from the *Dreams Can Come True* video? Let **Mellissa**, **Dan**, and **Laura** tell you their stories of abundance.

Life Lesson 10

Life Lesson 10

Appreciation

Is there a creative person whom you look up to? Who is it? Why? Do you have several creative heroes/heroines? It's always a good idea to have role models. They can show us the way. They can mentor us. We don't have to reinvent the wheel if they have done something similar along the way.

I have a friend who is a great grandmother. Her great grandson is nine months old. The baby was sitting on his dad's lap as his dad changed his password on the computer. The father started chatting with his wife as the baby played on the computer. Would you believe the baby changed the password? The creative self will come out to play even at an early age. It's nice to appreciate the talents of others, don't you think? How about you? Whom do you most appreciate?

How are you doing? Life can be tense at times and I hope you are hanging in there. One exercise I like to do around this time is to suggest that my students expect surprises every day. I know that this suggestion may sound ridiculously hokey, but it works! And when it does, it makes me feel so good. I have had whole classes join me in this exercise and it's amazing to hear about all the surprises.

It's very simple. Every day for a month, I expect a surprise. I don't put any conditions on the surprises. I just expect something wonderfully surprising to happen to me each day. Just expecting surprises makes me feel good! Then I write each surprise down. Some days I get more than one surprise. Some days I get big ones and some days I get small ones. I don't care about the size or how unique the surprise is. I just want to feel good. The fun part is that each time I do this exercise, amazing surprises come to me. I sometimes receive bonus checks and lucrative business sales out of the blue. I've met famous personalities and have been offered new and exciting opportunities while doing this exercise. If you like surprises, you might like to try expecting daily surprises and then share with others some of your surprising results.

Each day we learn more and more about ourselves. Start noticing, right now, how much more you know about yourself than yesterday. Keep your focus on appreciating yourself and seeing yourself becoming more self-aware. Many believe that what you are thinking about you will get more of. What would you like more of in your life? Do you want more to worry about or more to enjoy? If you think about how special you are, you will become even more special.

Isn't it wonderful to think lovely thoughts about yourself that feel good? It's time to make appreciating yourself a daily habit. Are you finding ways to appreciate more in your life as suggested in Life Lesson 7? If you haven't tried that yet, now might be the time. As a creative being, we are different from those who are just doing their routines and who are not tuned in to their inner creative selves. Who in your daily encounters is likely to enjoy this idea of creating?

Our self-respect can come from doing our creative work. Have you noticed that we sometimes need extra support during our creative periods? Have you found that boredom can sometimes drive you crazy? There is a connection between self-nurturing and self-respect. Watch for allowing yourself to be bullied by other people's ideas of what you should be doing. Don't sell yourself short. So what if they like you better if you follow their wishes? What about your own dreams and goals and desires? You don't want to fall into the self-disgust trap because you followed others' dreams instead of your own.

Cutting off my creative urges makes me unhappy and miserable. Letting the creativity flow makes me feel lighter than air. Appreciate your own uniqueness. Allow yourself to play and have fun while you work on your goals. You can't kill your dreams. They will come back to tap you on the shoulder and remind you that they are still on the back burner. Have you ever read the poem "A Dream Deferred" by Langston Hughes? How would it feel to not have a dream come to fruition? What will happen if you don't realize your dream or dreams? Rather than thinking about the negative, how about imagining what it would feel like to have your dreams come true? What does that feel like? Can you feel that way right now? How good does that feel? If it doesn't feel good, switch the topic to something that does feel good. Many times envisioning our dreams makes us remember that we don't have them yet. That can feel sad. If that happens, focus on anything that makes you feel good. Feeling good brings more of feeling good. I'm sure you can agree that more of feeling good is just a wonderful place to be.

The more you love and appreciate yourself, the more you let that creative part of you out to play and the better life feels. And make it fun! That means you have to tell the critical voice to be quiet and find more ways to pat yourself on the back!

The last week is on its way. There will be a final wrap-up based on your journal writings. Do not read them yet—that's coming up soon.

Don't forget to complete the Book Reflections. Use the book if you need to. Enjoy!

Questions to Answer:

1. Were you able to write in your journal three times this week on three different days?

2. How about your play date? Are you planning anything special in the near future? Can you do an extra one this week?

3. Were you able to take fifteen minutes of complete and total relaxation just for you each day? How many days this week did you do that?

4. Have any interesting surprises or opportunities come your way this week?

Please choose 8 out of the next 10 to answer:

5. What physical exercise do you need to do to be your personal best? Why?

6. List three ways you are changing because of this creative process. How does it feel?

7. What are some habitual, daily ways in which you show yourself appreciation? List five of them.

8. Plan a week of self-appreciation play dates for the future. List one special, kind activity that you will do for yourself every single day of that week.

9. Have any negative thoughts come up lately about your plans? How can you reprogram them to be positive thoughts instead? What are they? Be very brief and to the point about the negative thoughts and be much more verbose about the positive.

10. If you are looking for a new way to write in your journal, try making lists like the one below. Complete the following as quickly as you can:

    I feel

    I need

    I adore

    I think

    I wouldn't like

    I would like

    I crave

    I can now

    I don't like

    I do like

    I really would love

    I remember fondly

    I want to repeat

    I want to learn

    I sincerely hope

    I truly believe

    I see clearly

    I so appreciate

    I willingly share

    I joyfully accept

I happily agree with

I look forward to

I am pleasantly surprised about

I cheerfully allow

I am

11. Describe someone or something that you didn't appreciate in the past that you have come to appreciate. What happened to change your mind?

12. What are three aspects of your personality that you especially appreciate?

13. What are three aspects about you that others especially appreciate?

14. Does your everyday self differ in any way from your online self? Why or why not? If it does, in what ways does it differ?

Questions for Discussion:

A. What is something fun that you did when you were a child that you would like to do again? Why?

B. What is something that you love to do that also builds self-confidence?

C. Describe a television show, movie, commercial, or video clip that makes you laugh.

D. What is a surprise that you would love to get?

Questions to Ponder:

Have you ever been truly taken by surprise?

Is there a surprise that you have a hard time believing you would get?

What more do you really want in your life?

Who else wants more in your life for you?

What dreams keep you going? Why?

How can you visualize what you want without feeling sad because you don't have it?

If you had a magic wand, what dream would you fulfill first?

What would come second?

Who do you most appreciate in your life?

Who most appreciates you?

It's time to watch the last three selections from the *Dreams Can Come True* video. After you listen to stories of appreciation from **Jeff** and **Sherry**, **David** will present *A Dream Relaxation*. Remember to relax and enjoy. What dreams have come true for you? What future dreams are you looking forward to?

Book Reflections

1. What is the significance of the title of Gordon MacKenzie's book, *Orbiting the Giant Hairball*? What does the title mean?

2. Name three lessons in creativity that you've learned from reading this book.

3. What do you believe is your creative masterpiece in life? Do you have more than one?

4. What bliss are you following right now? What does that look like for you?

5. What creative projects are you working on right now? Do you have any on the back burner?

6. What aspects of this book did you especially enjoy reading?

Life Lesson 11

Life Lesson 11

More Self-Awareness

We do know what we want, don't we? Our inner dreams will enfold once we allow them to. We have to have the courage to admit what they are. Sometimes that can be difficult. We might have to delve. Sometimes we feel resistant. It's by seeing what we don't enjoy that we can easily figure out what we would enjoy. There is a path for each of us. To find it we need to explore what it is we want and what it is we don't want. The more we pay positive attention to what we want, the more what we want will begin to appear in our lives. Sometimes we have to get out of our own way. See what you want and let the doors open. Sometimes the best action is taking no action. Just letting the idea simmer and cook can open doors, too. Creativity can have some winding roads to explore. That's OK. The light will shine on exactly what you need to do next.

We are supposed to want more. We are intended to create. You get rid of the old and you bring in the new. That's what life is all about. Doesn't life feel better when it's light, playful, and full of fun? Joy and freedom and having fun—doesn't that sound good to you? You can make your life like that. Remember to keep appreciating, no matter what. The more you are grateful and appreciative, the more people, places, and things to appreciate will come into your life. The more you worry, the more you will need to worry.

I heard a story about a famous marshal artist recently. At one point in his career, he had hurt his back. He was told by doctors that he would have trouble walking for the rest of his life and that he would never do martial arts again. He refused to believe the negative diagnosis and he rehabbed himself back to fighting capacity.

Have you heard the story about the man who was given six months to live? He quits his job and he buys a sailboat. Then he takes the family to sail around the world. Ten years later he's still alive, incredibly happy, and healthy.

Another powerful story comes from a former student who wanted others to know the miracle in her family. Here it is in her own words:

The most amazing memory that I have is the outcome of a very specific time. My youngest daughter had been diagnosed at the age of seven months with a very rare type of Leukemia. At first, she had less than a 30% chance of survival. I hated the fact that they used numbers/percentages to decide my daughter's fate. Within a few days, we found that her sister—who was just two years old—was a perfect match for a bone-marrow transplant. That moment itself was an amazing memory, because her percentage just jumped to 50%! When the percentages climbed, obviously, the numbers weren't so bad to hear. After many hours, days, months of numerous ups and downs; by far the best memory was that each year that passed, her percentages climbed and climbed until finally hitting 99.999% after five years.

She is now twenty-two years old; graduating from Colorado State University in December and starting the Nursing Program at Front Range Community College in January.

Are you ready to see your life in a more positive way? Are you ready to see your life through rose-colored glasses? If you keep saying that your life has been full of woe, it will probably continue to be full of woe. How about you begin to see your life from a different, more positive angle? There are always two sides to the coin. How about looking at some of the positive parts instead? The more positives you see in your life, the more positives you will attract. Perhaps you tell yourself that in the past it took time to find what you wanted. These days things are changing. I'm realizing that it's possible to find what I want more easily. I look forward to finding them. In the meantime, let's see how much fun we can have in our lives.

Get your mind off of anything negative that might pop up again while believing that your dreams and desires are possible. If and when your mind starts getting negative again, gently tell it to be quiet and switch over to your new, more positive way of thinking. Every day I do this about something in my life. The sooner I let go of the old negative ideas and see my new, feel-good ideas about the subject, the sooner what I want shows up in my life. Try it and have some fun with it.

For example, if you keep saying that friends aren't easy to find, they won't be easy to find! See if you can say something to yourself that feels better. Perhaps something like: "In the past I found friends. It wasn't always the easiest but I've learned so much about life and I know that it can be easier this time." Start picking out traits that you like in people and focus on them rather than focusing on what you don't like. Talking to yourself positively is called positive self-talk and it feels so much better than negative self-talk. Also, start treating yourself like your own best friend and, those who do the same, will gravitate towards you. If your demeanor projects the belief that it's hard to find friends, it will probably continue to be. Change that and your ideal friends will find you. They are out there waiting for you.

This is week 11 and do I have two introspective tasks for you! You will need a poster board or cardboard, glue, a stapler, and scissors. Find about ten to twenty magazines that you won't mind cutting up. Give yourself about thirty to forty minutes and collect any pictures that reflect your dreams. You can even go back to your dream container to find more pictures. This collage will represent your vision of where you want to go in life. You are to put lots of pictures of your dreams on a board arranging them in a way that makes you very happy. Now find a place you can put your dream poster where you will be able to see it every day. You might even want to repeat this exercise in several months or do one on just one aspect of a dream to be even more specific.

For those of you who no longer use print materials☺, yes, it's OK to use pictures from online sources that are in the public domain. I still want you to physically make a collage—so remember to print it out and put it someplace you can see it, preferably first thing in the morning and last thing at night.

I've done this exercise many times in my life. The fun part is looking at my collages years later. They are like maps of my life. So many of the pictures have come to me! Doing a project like this makes it easy to see what you want. Visualizing is a powerful tool. And seeing what you want can bring results. It's that self-fulfilling prophecy you read about before. If you constantly see yourself falling down stairs, you will probably do that. If you constantly see and feel yourself winning at whatever you are doing, you will probably do that. We have choices in how to think and feel. It can be pretty difficult to get rid of a negative thought. However, like turning on a light switch, you can begin to think of anything more positive instead. That's a good way to change your attitude.

Feeling lousy? Try doing or thinking of something that makes you feel a bit better and keep doing or thinking about it. We can soothe ourselves and make ourselves feel better. Some could do this easily as children. You can recapture this skill as adults, if you want to. The CEO of a company doesn't usually get there by chance. He or she had a vision. What's your vision?

Questions to Answer:

1. Did you write three pages on three different days this week? Do you know anyone else who also keeps a journal?

2. How was your play date this week? What did you do? Have you considered doing a full day of play?

3. Were you able to take fifteen minutes of complete and total relaxation just for you each day? How many days this week did you do that?

4. Do remember to make the collage and put it in a special place for you to see each day. Describe it in detail and take a picture of it. Where did you put it?

Please choose 8 out of the next 10 to answer:

5. Have you been keeping track of surprises in your life? Have you noticed any special ones lately that you would like to write about?

6. Remember your self-portrait at the beginning of this book? Please make another one on a separate paper and compare the two. Describe any changes you might see. Why do you think that is?

7. Where is your favorite place to live: the city, the country, or the suburbs? Why?

8. What kind of décor do you like? Where is a room decorated just the way you like it? Describe it. Why do you like it so much?

9. Describe your ideal adventure. Where would it be and what would you do?

10. Make or buy something delicious to eat. What did you have? Why did you pick those foods?

11. Give yourself twenty minutes this week to listen to music and do something zany. Twenty minutes can refresh you. Enjoy! What music did you listen to? One of my former students put on her wedding gown (veil and all) and vacuumed her home while she listened to her favorite tunes. What did you do?

12. When was the last time you really had fun—the kind of fun that keeps you smiling all day long? Describe it.

13. How much of your day are you actually enjoying and having fun? 10%? 30%? 75%? 90%? How could you increase your percentage to make your life even more fun?

14. If you could plan the perfect surprise party for yourself, what would it be like? Who would you invite and where would it be? Please write out all the details.

Questions for Discussion:

A. If you could invent your own holiday, what would it be called and how would you celebrate it?

B. Make believe you just discovered a new star. What would it look like? What would you name it and why?

C. You've been asked to name a sports team. What sport would it be and what would the uniforms look like?

D. Do you have a nickname that you like being called? If you don't have one or if you have one you don't like, is there a nickname you would like to have?

Questions to Ponder:

How can you let more fun into your life?

How can you allow your creative self to play even more?

Are you now your own best friend?

Are you trusting yourself more and more?

What new ideas are you visualizing for yourself?

Have you found any new insights lately?

How can you care for yourself even more?

Are you enjoying writing in your journal?

Why or why not?

How can you enjoy writing to yourself even more?

Have you seen any films that have made you feel more self-aware?

Life Lesson 12

Life Lesson 12

Final Overview and Ending Thoughts

Do enjoy your final wrap-up! You have three choices. Here they are:

Read your journal pages! Write yourself a letter describing how it felt to do this and what you discovered about yourself. Do include those positive actions and ideas you most appreciate. Make this letter a heartfelt treasure that you can keep to reread and cherish.

OR

Read your journal pages! With a highlighter, highlight only the positive entries. Read your journal a second time and read only what is highlighted. What would you like the next three months of your life to be like? Describe that in a heartfelt letter to yourself that you can keep to reread and cherish.

OR

Do not read your journal pages! Put your journal away to possibly read at a future time. Describe how you would like the next three months of your life to be in a heartfelt letter to yourself that you can keep to reread and cherish.

Questions to Answer:

1. How many days did you write this week? Are you thinking about continuing with your journal writing? Why or why not?

2. What did you do on your play date this week? You were supposed to enjoy twelve play dates. Do you plan on continuing this exercise? Why or why not?

3. Were you able to take fifteen minutes a day to fully and deeply relax?

4. Did anything happen this week that surprised or inspired you in a special way?

5. Are you excited about pursuing the creative ideas that are now on your agenda? If not, what can you do to generate excitement?

6. What aspects of this book will you continue to incorporate in your life?

Questions for Discussion:

A. If you could buy any car that you wanted, what would it be and why? What color would it be?

B. What is so very wonderful about your life right now?

C. What is the URL to a video clip that makes you feel inspired and hopeful? What do you like about it?

D. What would you like people to remember about you when you are gone?

The Last Question to Ponder:

How can you and your creative self continue to have a wonderfully positive relationship?

Ending Thoughts:

In Life Lesson 7, you compiled some future goals for yourself. Your creative self will guide you towards the goals you really want to achieve. Pay attention to them. If you try to forget them, the thought of not achieving what you want will come knocking on your door when you least expect it. Let your creative self point the way. Remember, you don't have to be perfect. The more you use your imagination to see how you would like your life to be, the more you can create those pleasing paths that will lead you to where you want to go. Life then feels less risky and more secure. If you let your creative self help along the way, you will find more and more opportunities wherever you look. The whole idea is to ***enjoy the journey***! There will always be more goals, more ideas, and more life events to strive for. Find fun ways to enjoy every minute of the planning, the dreaming, and the traveling along the path to what you want. Don't forget to make it fun!

I want you all to have a lovely time now that you are finished. Plan to play as much as possible! That's your task. Keep appreciating every minute. Enjoy as much of your life as you can. Play! Have fun! Appreciate yourself and others. Keep enjoying the positive in life and make lemonade whenever you are handed lemons. Don't let anyone convince you that life is not supposed to be joyful. We can find a way to make life a delicious adventure, if we let ourselves. Enjoy every minute! Don't waste your energy on sweating the small stuff.

Remember that there's a magic to believing. Remember that the more you appreciate and enjoy the good stuff in life, the more you will see to appreciate and enjoy. Make lists of wonderful events and surprises. You deserve to feel good. You are in charge of how you feel. You can feel good no matter what. Don't skimp on giving yourself time to enjoy you. You are a wonderful creator. Take out that magic wand of positive thinking and let it flow. Others will marvel at how happy and fulfilled you are. It's a continuing process. Don't get stuck—keep it flowing. You know how to make yourself feel good. You can do it. There are lots of options in life. Appreciate whenever you can. Don't get caught up in the negative and the hustle and bustle. It's your life—how do you want to live it? Enjoy every second. Be your own best friend. Find ways to love yourself continually.

For your perusal, here is some of the feedback that I've given over the years:

Whenever I feel guilt, it's time to make myself feel better. I tell myself that life can get better and better and that good things can happen all around me. Pretty soon I am actually noticing that life is getting better and the good things begin to multiply. You deserve the good stuff so get ready to receive it!

Our creative selves come out to play all the time. However, sometimes we are nowhere in the vicinity to play with them. If we are worried or upset or frustrated or angry, we're not going to be making much contact. If we are relaxed or happy or joyful, now we can make the rendezvous. We don't have to work hard for this. We have to let go. So that's why there are play dates. Relax and take it easy. Feel really good and see what happens then!

Each day we learn more and more about ourselves. Start noticing, right now, how much more you know about yourself than yesterday. Keep appreciating yourself and seeing yourself becoming more self-aware.

By the way, there are always more dreams to imagine. I believe we can accomplish so very many no matter what others tell us. Life is amazing when we let it be. Start getting excited about the possibilities!

Everything is easier when you look back. If we could have done it differently in the past, we would have. In the present we have more information so it's easier to say that we should have done something differently. I think we have to stop "shoulding" on ourselves. It's just not fair.

How nice to be doing what you enjoy. Wouldn't it be lovely never to have to do anything we didn't enjoy? Of course, we can always change our opinions about what we like or don't like.

Daydreaming can help you to get in focus. How do you want something to turn out? See it the way you want and believe it can happen. Get rid of any thoughts that what you want can't possibly happen for you.

The impossible has happened for many who believed it could happen. Cancer cured. Wheelchairs no longer needed. Relationships saved. Prosperity, fame, and good fortune found. The same is true for the negative, however. So we might as well use the self-fulfilling prophecy for the positive rather than the negative.

The more we see the positive in others, the more positive there is to see. Keep looking at the good and more good comes into our lives. Life just happens that way. They say that we get more of what we are thinking about and feeling. Can we feel good even in the midst of bad things happening? That's a tough one; however, I know I can always feel better just by altering my thoughts.

There's always the creative trick—it's how to enjoy the ride even at the times when it's bumpy! You might keep asking how you can make lemonade out of whatever feels like lemons. Those lemons are there to lead us to the next step. What we don't want can point the way to what we do want. The lemons can be good for us when we allow them to lead us. It doesn't always feel good so we have to figure out ways to accept it and go on. Once you do that, everything tends to fall into place.

The more you appreciate and enjoy what you do have, more of that will then show up in your life. It's like we look at the world with glasses colored with what we are thinking. A little attitude tweaking and we turn our lives around.

One way to feel better is to keep appreciating and admiring what others have. More appreciation and less jealousy attracts in more of what they have for you.

Can you change the idea of should do into want to do? We can generate enthusiasm for anything. Good for you when you do! Please continue to be selfish and spend even more time with yourself whenever you can. Consider it the ultimate homework.

Every time that inner critic starts bothering you, can you switch the thought to something else? Or can you do something that will take your mind off of the negativity? We don't deserve to be hard on ourselves for anything. Now that's easy for me to write and not always easy to do. Start planning your substitution thoughts and actions and then get ready to feel much better!

Sometimes we need to talk about something negative if, by talking about it, it will make us feel better. Do we get relief and feel better? Then the talking is good and we can get on with other things. If we feel worse, then that's not the best thing to do. The question then becomes, can you tell when to talk about it and when not to?

Creativity is embedded in your core. It makes you—you. You are your own creative endeavour. It sounds like you are right in the middle of truly appreciating your own abilities. Shakespeare wrote, "The readiness is all." Are you ready?

It's you who is doing the changing and growing. There's that saying, "The only thing constant in life is change." The more we keep focusing on the good changes, the more the good stuff comes to us.

Hope is a big motivator. If you hope that all will be well, it feels better than worrying about what to do if it doesn't. Most of what we worry about never even happens.

You are the most important person in your life. You can become your own best friend. Only you know what is truly good for you. Others can guess, but you are the source of that information. You can't lose when you take care of you.

We don't need to people please by showing others more of who we are when we don't want to do that. Taking care of yourself is a wonderful thing to do.

I think it's really important to always listen to your gut. Our inner voice speaks to us and guides us. Unfortunately most of us have several voices from our past that like to chatter. So it's good to know which voice is the inspirational one!

Worrying is visualizing the negative solution rather than the positive solution. We can reprogram ourselves. Please don't say or think, "I don't test well." Put that idea in the past. That was the past. Focus on the possibilities of doing better on the next test and see what happens.

They say that what other people think of us is none of our business. That's a tough one, but let's face it, if someone doesn't like or respect me, there are lots who do. Meantime, life is too short not to be fun. Find ways to make it fun, even when it doesn't feel good. Changing lemons to lemonade is a good game to play and it brings more great stuff into our lives.

Each of us is special and important and unique. We have to put ourselves first or else we might not have anything to give to anyone else. Some of us were taught to put ourselves last and to cater to others first. It just takes practice to love ourselves and treat ourselves like we are the special people we are. It's just not healthy for us to hide our lights. We are each unique and wonderful. There will never be another you! It's time to celebrate ourselves!

If you notice how you are 1% healthier and happier each day, where will you be in one hundred days?

Stay as excited as you can about life and all the wonderful things it has to offer. We are allowed to follow our dreams. We are allowed to enjoy every minute of the journey. Looking at life through rose-colored glasses is a lovely way to live. Keep your focus on the good stuff!

And now for my favorite homework assignment! It's called cartoon therapy and I like to pass this along to anyone who is injured or feeling sick or is just generally under the weather.

1. Change into pyjamas or sweats or anything comfortable.
2. Get a warm and comfortable blanket and lie on the couch.
3. Turn on the television and watch your favorite cartoons or children's show—my favorite is *Scooby-Doo.*
4. Take a break for either hot soup or cereal—whichever sounds best to you.
5. Do this for as long as you like. I swear that doing this assignment always makes me feel better shortly afterwards!

Bibliography

Adler, Ron and Towne, Neil. *Looking Out, Looking In.* Belmont, CA: Wadsworth Publishing Company, 2006.

Allen, James. *As a Man Thinketh.* Willa Park, IL: Cornerstone Books, 1902.

Butterworth, Eric. "Eric Butterworth Collection." Unity. Accessed February 4, 2013. http://www.unity.fm/program/Butterworth.

Cameron, Julia. *The Artist's Way.* New York: Penguin, 2002.

Campbell, Joseph with Bill Moyers. *The Power of Myth.* New York: Bantam Doubleday Dell Publishing, 1988.

Canfield, Jack and Wells, Harold. *100 Ways to Enhance Self-Concept in the Classroom.* Englewood Cliffs, NJ: Prentice-Hall, 1976.

Carnegie, Dale. *How to Stop Worrying and Start Living.* New York: Simon and Schuster, 1985.

Dyer, Wayne. *Your Erroneous Zones.* New York: HarperCollins, 1991.

Gawain, Shakti. *Creative Visualization.* Novato, CA: New World Library, 2002.

Hay, Louise, perf. *Receiving Prosperity.* Carlsbad: Hay House, Inc., 2005, compact disc.

Hay, Louise. *The Power Is Within You.* Carlsbad: Hay House, 1997.

Hay, Louise. *You Can Heal Your Life.* Carlsbad: Hay House, Inc., 1984.

Hicks, Jerry and Esther. *Ask and it is Given.* Carlsbad: Hay House, Inc., 2004.

Hill, Napoleon. *Think & Grow Rich.* New York: Ballantine Books, 1983.

Mackenzie, Gordon. *Orbiting the Giant Hairball: A Corporate Fool's Guide to Surviving with Grace*. New York: Penguin Putnam, 2002.

Murnaw, Stefan and Oldfield, Wendy. *Caffeine for the Creative Mind*. Cincinnati: F + W Publications, Inc., 2006.

Ponder, Catherine. *Open Your Mind to Receive*. Marina Del Rey, CA: DeVorss & Company, 1983.

Warren, Neil Clark. *Make Anger Your Ally*. Colorado Springs: Focus on the Family Publishing, 1990.

Wangchuck, Jigme Singye. Quoted in "Gross National Happiness." The Permanent Mission of the Kingdom of Bhutan to the United Nations in New York. Accessed February 5, 2013. http://www.un.int/bhutan/bhutan/gross-national-happiness.

Here I am. This is proof that my creative self liked to have fun even at an early age!

Also by Janet Scarpone:

Learn Math Quickly

Learn Oral Communication Quickly

Learn Writing & Grammar Quickly

Dreams Can Come True

www.learnquickly.com

Printed in the United States
By Bookmasters